Simply Joplin

The Music of Scott Joplin
12 of His Ragtime Classics
Arranged by Mary K. Sallee

Simply Joplin is a collection of the most popular piano solos—two-steps, waltzes, and rags—by Scott Joplin (1868–1917). These pieces have been carefully selected and arranged by Mary K. Sallee for Easy Piano, making many of Joplin's most charming rags accessible to pianists of all ages. Phrase markings, articulations, fingering and dynamics have been included to aid with interpretation, and a large print size makes the notation easy to read.

Scott Joplin lived at the turn of the 20th century, and many consider him the "King of Ragtime." His immensely popular "Maple Leaf Rag," published in 1899, made him famous and helped elevate ragtime to a respected musical genre. Joplin's rags are known for their singing right-hand melodies, dancing left-hand accompaniments, and playful syncopations. They also fused the traditions of Romantic piano playing with elements of African-American folk music. Additionally, most of his rags contain a variety of sections, allowing the player to experience contrast in key and character within each work.

Joplin was inducted into the Songwriting Hall of Fame. He was posthumously awarded the Pulitzer Prize for his contribution to American music. Additionally, "The Entertainer" was featured in the 1973 Academy Award-winning film *The Sting*. For all of these reasons and many more, his music is exciting to explore.

After all, he is *Simply Joplin!*

D1716783

Copyright © MMVIII by ALFRED MUSIC
All rights reserved
ISBN-10: 0-7390-5018-4
ISBN-13: 978-0-7390-5018-7

Alfred

Contents

Bethena
(A Concert Waltz)
(1905)

Music by Scott Joplin
Arranged by Mary K. Sallee

A Breeze from Alabama

(A Ragtime Two-Step)

Music by Scott Joplin
Arranged by Mary K. Sallee

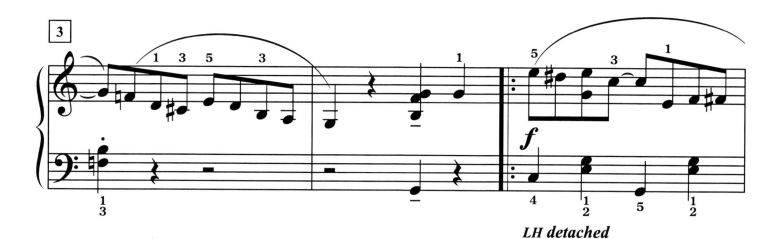

LH detached

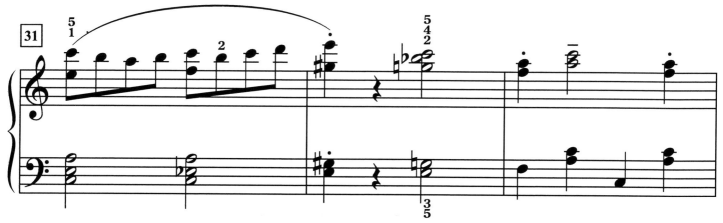

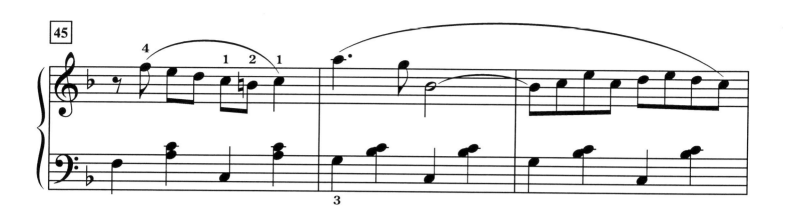

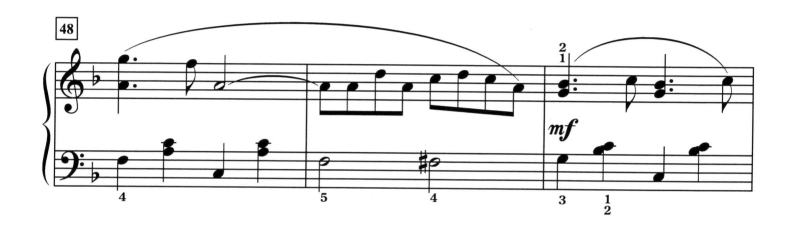

14

The Easy Winners

(A Ragtime Two-Step)

Music by Scott Joplin
Arranged by Mary K. Sallee

LH detached

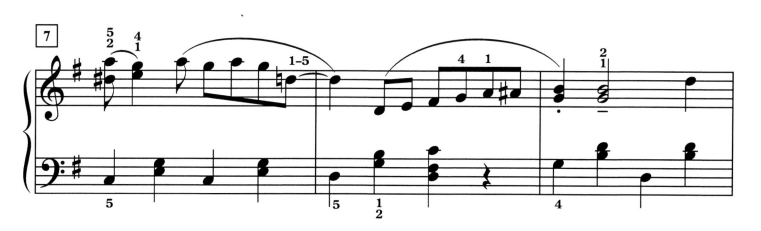

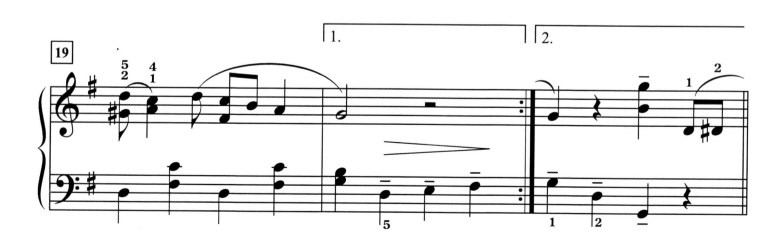

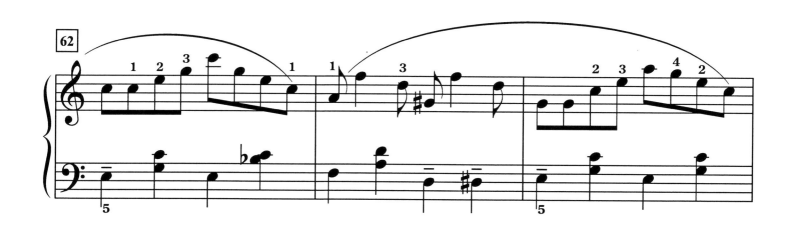

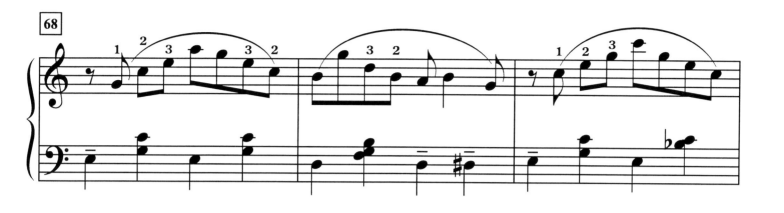

The Entertainer

Music by Scott Joplin
Arranged by Mary K. Sallee

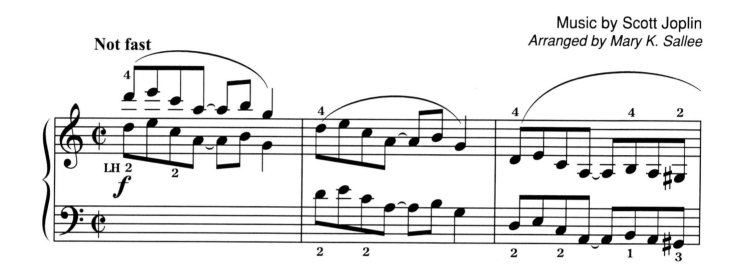

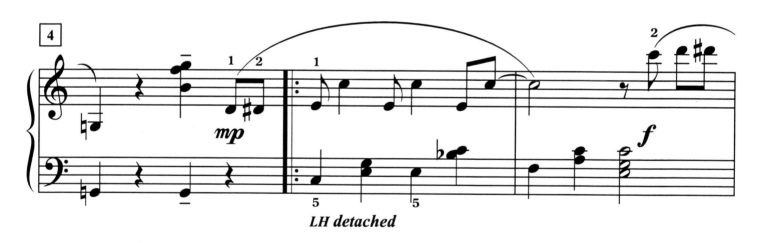

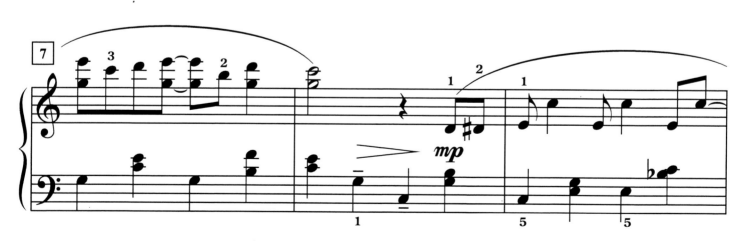

24

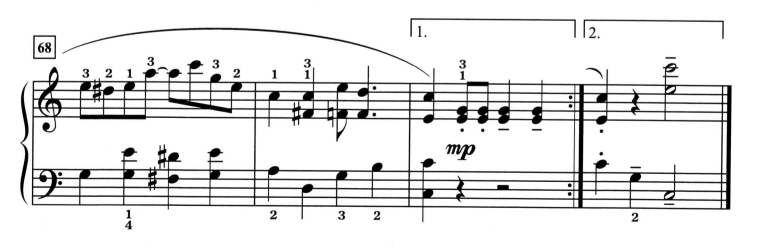

The Chrysanthemum

Music by Scott Joplin
Arranged by Mary K. Sallee

Slow march tempo

LH detached

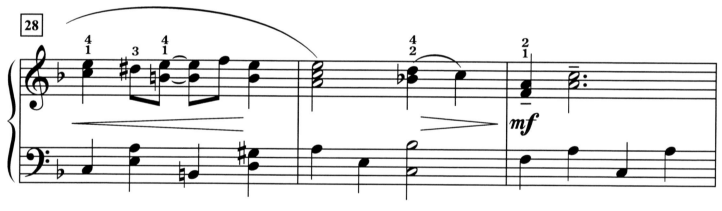

The Nonpareil
(A Rag and Two-Step)

Music by Scott Joplin
Arranged by Mary K. Sallee

Slow march tempo

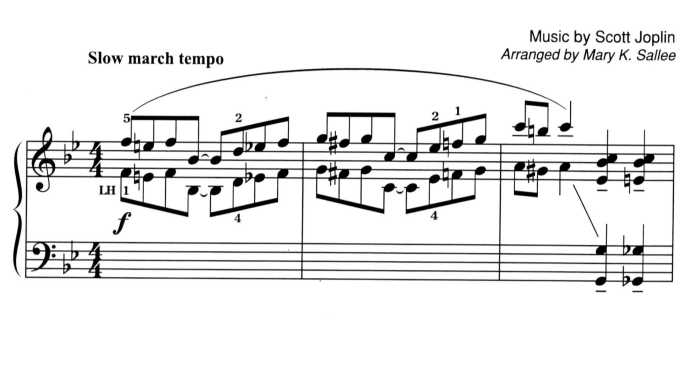

LH detached

Original Rags

Music by Scott Joplin
Arranged by Mary K. Sallee

Moderato

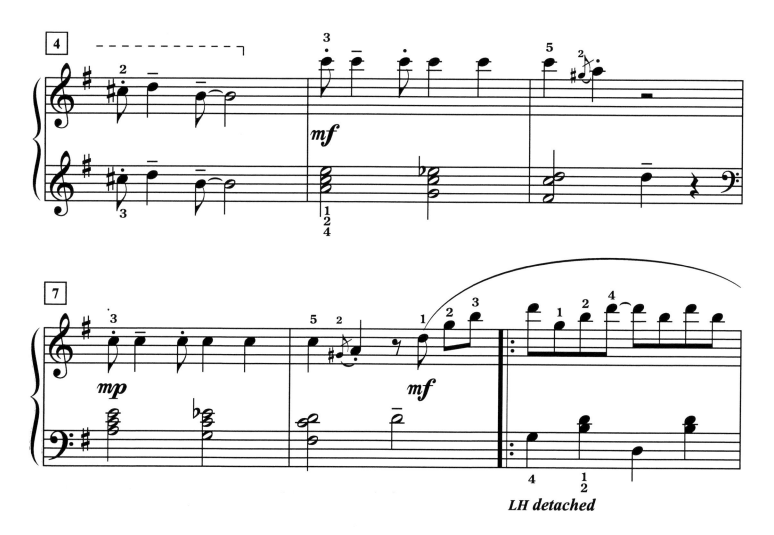

LH detached

42

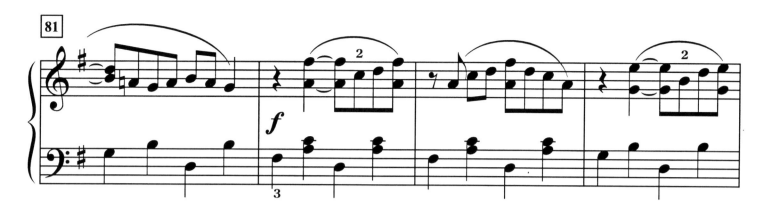

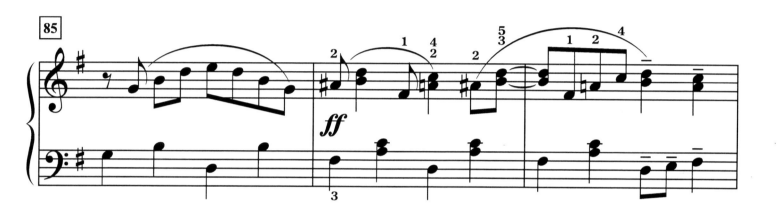

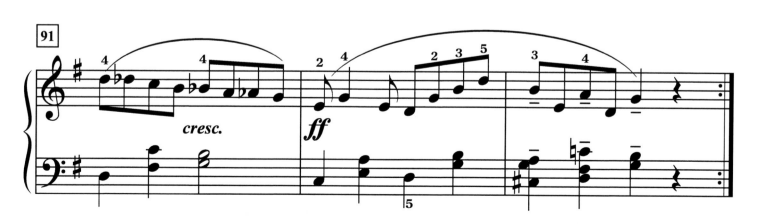

Peacherine Rag

Music by Scott Joplin
Arranged by Mary K. Sallee

Not too fast

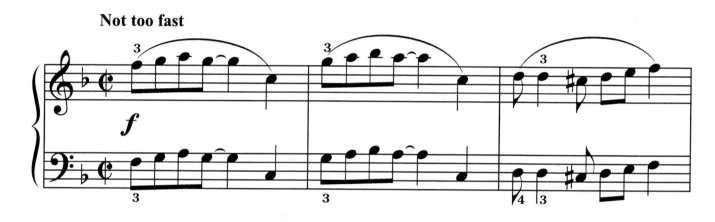

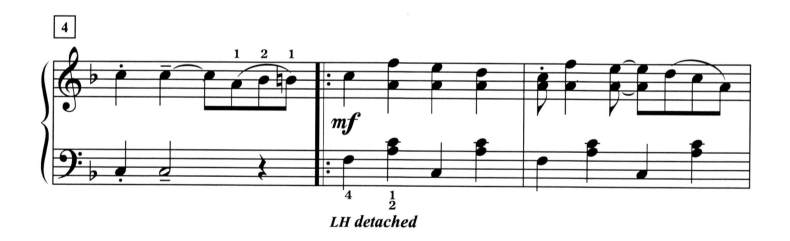

LH detached

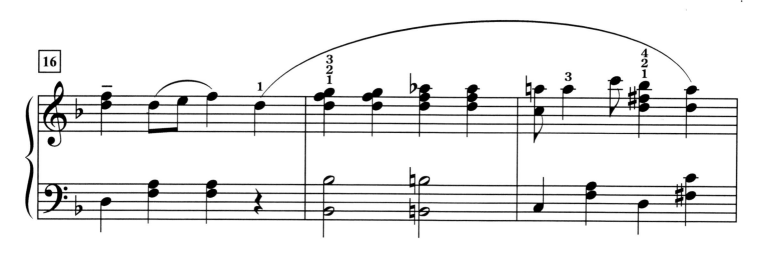

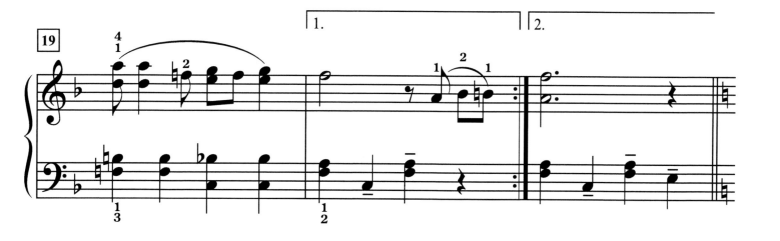

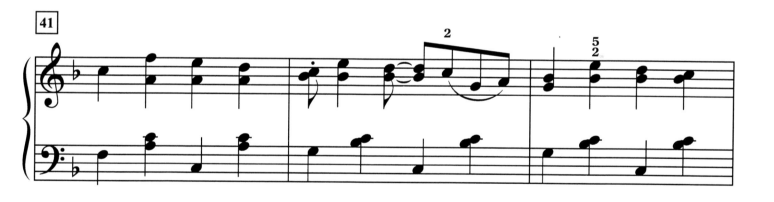

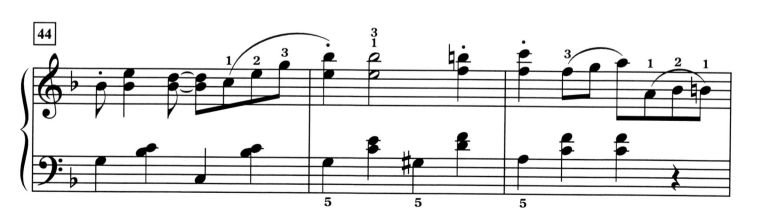

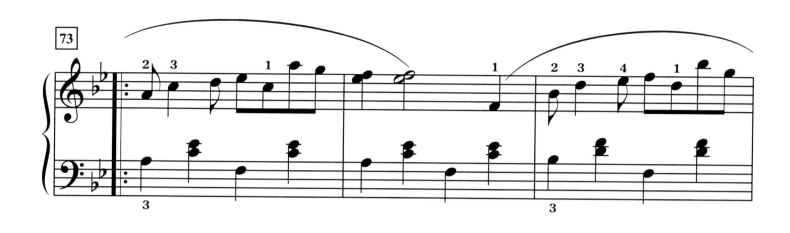

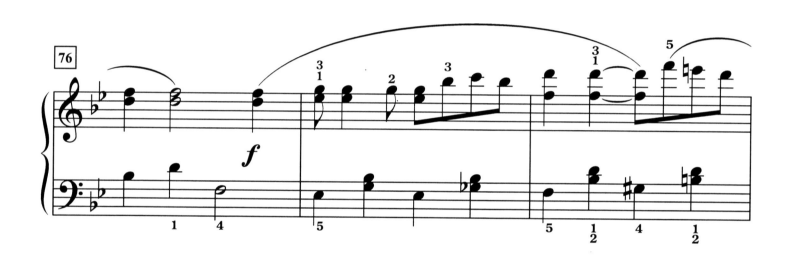

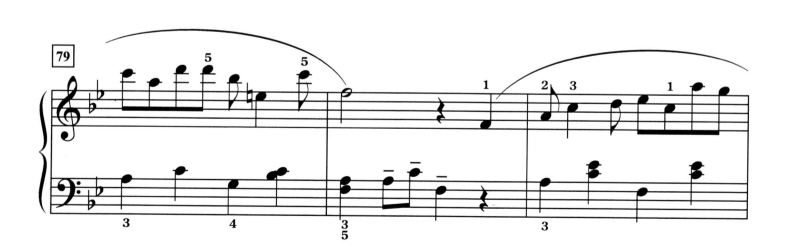

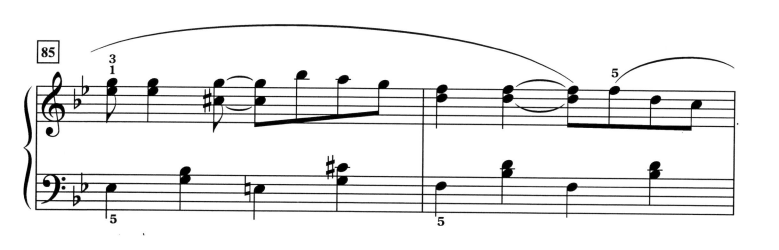

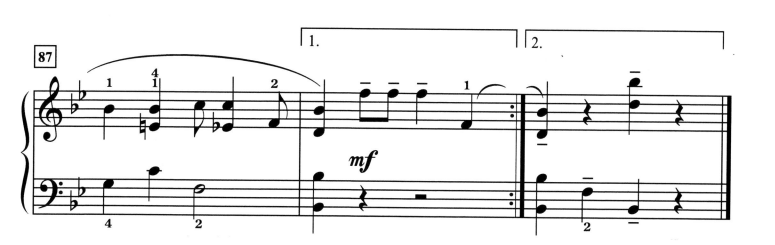

Ragtime Dance

(A Stop-Time Two-Step)

Music by Scott Joplin
Arranged by Mary K. Sallee

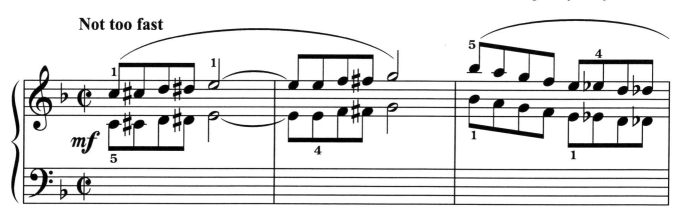

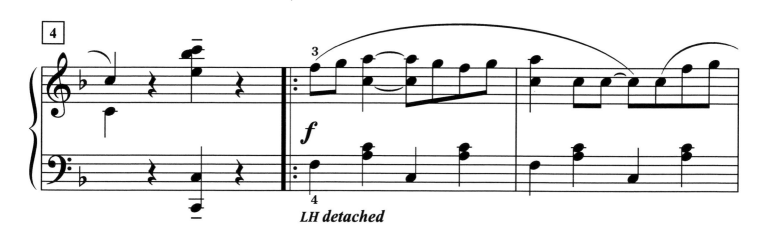

LH detached

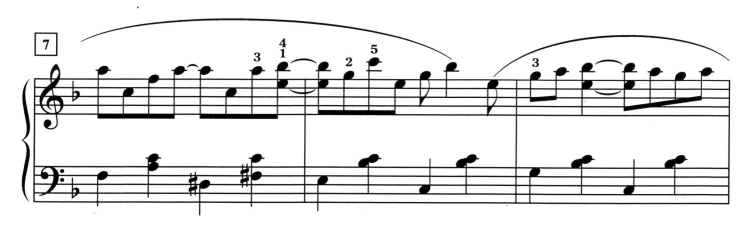

58

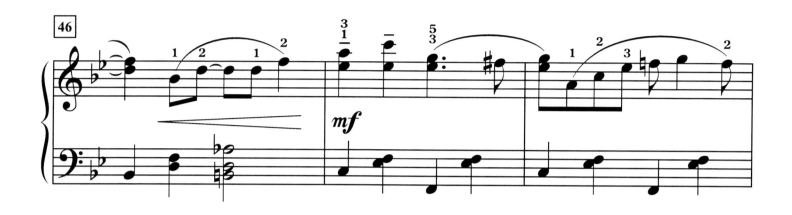

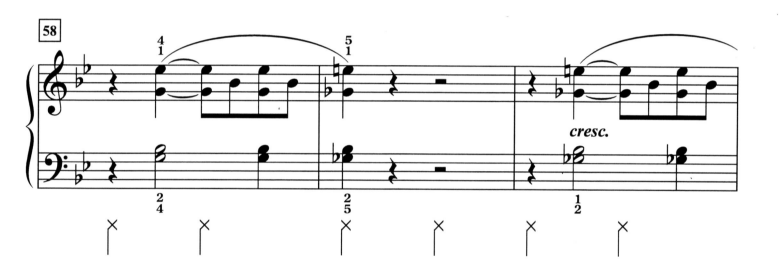

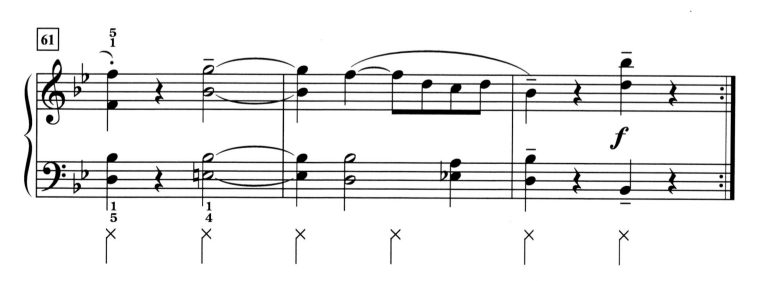

* For each ✕, stamp the heel of one foot on the floor.

62

Solace
(A Mexican Serenade)
(1909)

Music by Scott Joplin
Arranged by Mary K. Sallee

Very slow march time

both hands sempre legato

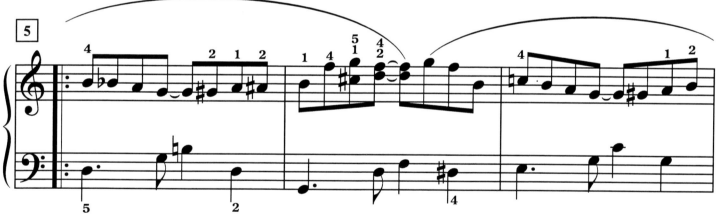

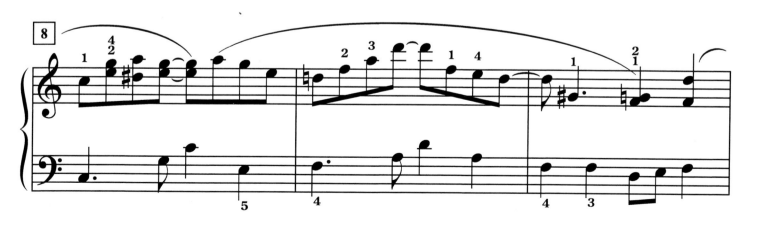

Weeping Willow

(A Ragtime Two-Step)

Music by Scott Joplin
Arranged by Mary K. Sallee

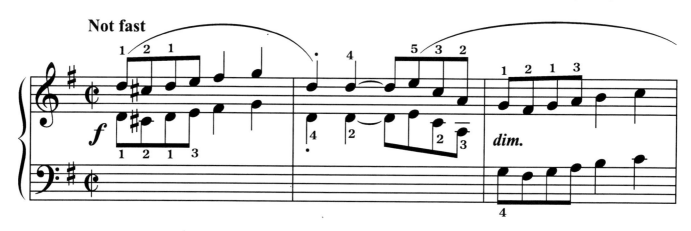

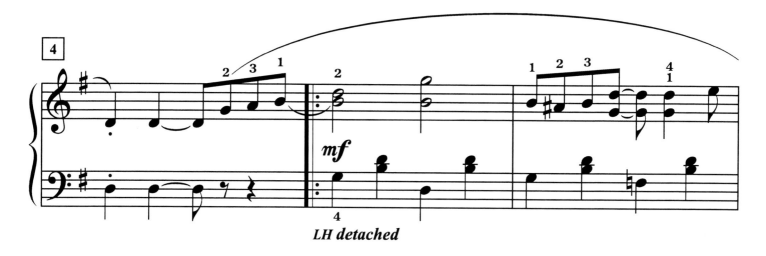

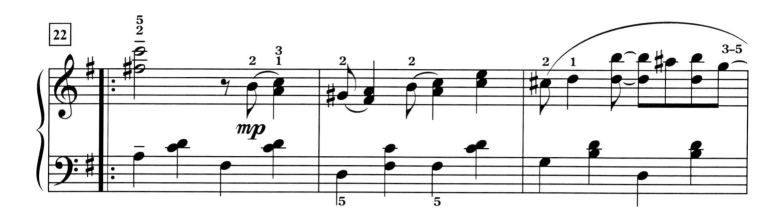

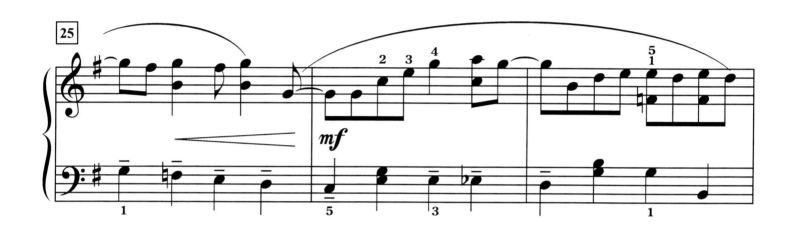

Maple Leaf Rag

Music by Scott Joplin
Arranged by Mary K. Sallee

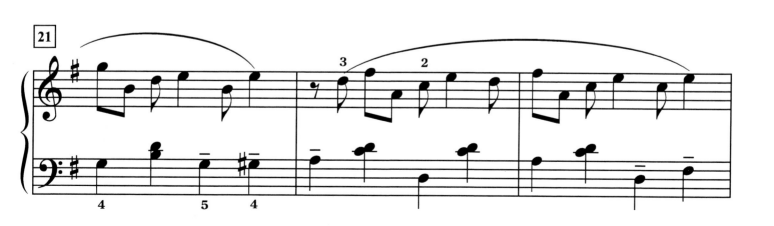